Straight From My Uncensored Heart

By

LaShawn D. Childs

First published by AuthorHouse 06/09/04

ISBN: 1-4184-5788-4 (e-book)
ISBN: 1-4184-3823-5 (Paperback)

Library of Congress Control Number: 2003098567

This book is printed on acid free paper.

Printed in the United States of America
Bloomington, IN

CONTENTS

ACKNOWLEDGMENTS

First of all, I would like to give thanks to my almighty God who is the head of my life. I thank Him for His forgiving power and for having mercy on me when my life was out of control. I thank Him for giving me another chance to surrender to His will. I thank God for delivering me from the death grip of sin. I promised Him that since He allowed me to live that I would share my story of His goodness and mercy through poetry.

I would like to thank my family, friends, and church family for encouraging me to write this book. A special thank you goes out to my sisters for all of their help and support. They listened every time the Lord gave me another poem. They were so excited when I told them that I was finally going to publish that they immediately began my marketing campaign. I want to thank Big B who also listened to the poems and for sharing her excitement through tears. I want to thank my mother who critiqued and praised my work. She researched and recommended several publishers. Thank you for planting a financial seed in order for my book to be published. I want to thank my father for encouraging me to publish while the book was fresh on my heart. I also want to thank him for carrying around some of the special poems in his shirt pocket.

I want to thank the Whites for being my closest friends. Thank you for pointing me to Jesus when I did not know how to get to Him myself. Thank you for the cherished memories that will always remain in my heart. Most of all, thank you for accepting me, believing in me, and reassuring me that I can fly.

Last but not least, I want to thank my husband. Thank you for entering my life at the end of this book. Thank you for starting chapter one of my next book. Thank you for praying this book into completion. Thank you for being my king, my best friend, and a wonderful father to our children. I love you.

FORWARD

God says all of the big words in our lives; however, it is often times that the little words make the big words sing. LaShawn is a rare and welcomed talent who is dedicated to the word made flesh. She is also a spellbinding spinner of such small words that ornament God's word.

I first met LaShawn in Emporia, Kansas in 1990. It was during that time that I discovered a young woman, who without knowing it then, was being put on the Potter's wheel to be shaped into a vessel that God could use for such a time as this. One of Shawn's first questions to me was, "How will I know when God speaks to me?" My answer to her was simply, "You will just know." I believe that as you read her book, you will say like I did, that Shawn has truly heard God's voice. She has done a masterful job of putting her feelings and expressions on paper. As you travel along this journey, you will be able to see that through our mess ups that God continues to clean up. In this book, you will be able to review a heart that has been exposed, uncensored, and freed to share the love of God and the forgiveness of Jesus Christ. So, sit back in a warm place and open your heart and let God display a work of peace, joy, and love.

Shawn, remember that through the writing of this book of poetry that God has truly made you a woman of beauty, grace, and of character. Keep growing, glowing, and showing the world that it is no secret what God can do. It has been a long time coming and as a result of your obedience, I believe that God is saying that you can fly.

Delmar A. White

INTRODUCTION

I invite you to open up your mind and come along with me into a journey of my heart. When I was growing up, I experienced some traumatic situations early in life. Due to my fear and pain, I did not feel comfortable expressing my true thoughts and feelings. Unfortunately, I learned the hard way that it was not healthy to keep my emotions bottled up on the inside. When I decided to deal with some of my issues, it seemed easier to express myself by writing instead of talking. As I matured, I realized that God had blessed me with the gift of writing poetry. After much prayer and some deep soul-searching, I have been delivered from the bondage of fear of communicating and expressing myself to others. Since those chains have been broken, I have been commissioned to share my gift with you. I pray that something that you encounter while on this journey will be a blessing to you.

CHAPTER ONE

GLORIFYING HIS HOLY NAME

LOOKING AT JESUS CHRIST

Just looking back over my life,
Experienced pain, heartache, and strife.
Saw the hand of Jesus deliver me out,
Up out of my bondage, it was Him, no doubt.
Safe in His arms, He wanted me to rest,
Cried out to Him so that I could stand the test.
He heard my cry and wiped my tears,
Reached out to me and took away my fears.
I tried everything else and it seemed to fail,
Surrendered my will and now I have a story to tell.
Thank you Lord for saving me from a burning hell.

GOD IS SO GOOD

If I had 10,000 tongues,
I could not tell it all.
Not only is God good to me
but He is good to each one of you all.
When I think of His goodness
and what He has done for me,
I have to lift my hands in praise
because I get so happy.
You do not know
where He has brought me from.
There have been so many ways made for me
that I cannot remember some.
I cannot begin to tell you
how He takes care of me.
He is better than any of the rest
and is as sweet as He can be.
I can tell you without shame
what type of lover He can be.
He loves me so much
that He gave His life for me.
I can tell you that He promised
to supply all of my needs.
He said it in His word
and all I have to do is believe.
I can tell you with assurance
that He cannot tell a lie.
Everything that He says,
I know that it will fly.
I always thought
that I knew how to be loved.
I never knew
that true love comes from above.
God has been
so good to me.
Try Him for yourself
and you can taste and see.

HE IS WORTHY

Jesus means the world to me.
I never knew how deep His love could be.
He showed up for me countless times this year.
He spoke to me constantly and made sure that I could hear.
He kept the enemy at bay so many times,
just when I thought I was going to lose my mind.
He forgave and cleansed me and gave me another chance.
He was my partner when it was time to dance.
He was my lover when it was time to make love.
He showed me that real love comes from above.
He held me and rocked me in His loving arms.
He charged His angels to protect me from danger and harm.
I love Him and praise Him because He is so good to me.
All I can say is hallelujah because He is so worthy.

GOD IS

Actively pursuing me Alpha Almighty Always thinking about me
Burden-bearer Battle-fighter Beginning Bright and morning star
Counselor Creator Comforter Compassionate Courteous Coming back
Does not slumber nor sleep Doctor Desires praise Divine Deep
Everlasting Everywhere Exciting Everything to me Extreme End
Forgiving Faithful Father Fearless Friend Faster than immediately
God all by himself Gentle Giving Good Great I Am Good listener
Healer Heart-fixer Holy Heavenly Father Holy Spirit Holy Ghost
Intelligent Important Intimate In-control In-charge Instant I Am
Jehovah Jirah Jealous Just a prayer away Joy-giver Jesus Christ Just
King of kings Keeper of my soul Keen Kind
Life-giver Lamb of God Lord of lords Light Lawyer Love
Marvelous Mighty Mind-regulator Magnificent Merciful Master
Never fails Never lies Never leaves nor forsakes me
Omnipresent Omnipotent Omniscient Owns the cattle on 1000 hills
Prince of peace Perfect Powerful Passionate Present Possessive
Quiet voice Quick to listen Quick to save Quality Quantity
Righteous Real Rich in houses and land Rock Relief Ruler Royal
Son of God Shelter Savior Sweet Supreme Strong-tower Shepherd
Trinity Trustworthy Tear-wiper Teacher Truth
Understanding Ultimate Unique
Very near Valuable Victorious
Way-maker Wheel in the middle of the wheel Wonderful Wise the Word
X-cellent friend X-cellent lover X-cellent counselor X-cellent father
Yearning for me Yoke is easy Yahweh
Zest Zeal

FATHER GOD

Thank you Lord for one more day
and for the strength to go on my way.
Thank you Lord for protecting me
and for keeping me as safe as I can be.
Thank you Lord for one more chance
and for letting me see You at a glance.
Thank you Lord for dying for my sins
without a "maybe" or "depends".
Thank you Lord for my health
and for sharing our Father's wealth.
Thank you Lord for being so good
and for blessing me like You said You would.

I JUST WANTED YOU TO KNOW

I just wanted You to know that I think You are the best.
You are better to me than any of the rest.
The thing that I love most about You,
is that You are always with me and I know this is true.
You go before and behind me and You never leave me alone.
It does not matter if I am caught up in something or on the telephone.
You are so sweet to me and I love to hear You speak.
I hear You loud and clear and in Your word I seek.
I am grateful that You always have time for me.
You are very attentive and never too busy.
Thank you for taking care of me and providing like You do.
Thank you for showing me that Your love is unconditional and true.
Thank you for being faithful and for being my number one man.
Thank you for holding and protecting me in Your right hand.
I love you Jesus.

REAL LOVE

Thank you Lord for showing me the real definition of love.
God is love and real love comes from above.
Real love was shown when You died upon the cross.
Real love was shown when You became my boss.
Real love was shown on a hill on Calvary.
Real love was shown when You died especially for me.
Real love was shown in the scars in Your hands.
Real love is shown in Your word so that I can understand.
Real love was shown when You forgave all of my sins.
Real love was shown when You laid down Your life for a friend.
Real love was shown when I surrendered everything to You.
Real love is shown when I walk and talk like You do.
Real love is knowing that You are God and I become still.
Real love is saying yes to Your will.

TO MY SWEETHEART ON VALENTINES DAY

I want to express myself to my man
to let You know that You are my number one fan.
Speaking of love, that is a deep subject, you see,
I am so in love with You and You are in love with me.
Out of all my past loves, You are the best.
You are much better than any of the rest.
You are faithful, caring, and ever so kind.
The depth of our relationship blows my mind.
I am grateful to have You as my best friend.
You promised to love me until the very end.
No one has ever respected me the way that You do.
I feel like a queen when I am with You.
No one has ever showered me with so many gifts
and when You present them, my spirits lift.
No one has ever protected me with such a strong arm.
When I am in Your presence, I will suffer no harm.
No one has ever spoken so sweetly to me.
The sound of Your voice is like a rich melody.
No one has ever been so loyal to me.
When I am in Your company, I feel like royalty.
No one has ever comforted me like You do.
No matter what the problem is, You always see me through.
I have never experienced real love before.
It is so satisfying that it makes me want more.
My life has changed and it is all because of You.
I could never imagine living my life without You.
I want You to know that I love You with all of my heart.
The love that we share will never part.
My heart and my soul belong to You.
I am blessed that our commitment is true.
I am honored that I am Your wife.
Jesus, You are the true love of my life.

SERVING GOD

If serving God was
food, would you be overweight?
money, would you be bankrupt?
a crime, would you be in jail?
clothes, would you be naked?
hot, would you be on fire?
water, would you be thirsty?
business, would you be the CEO?
cold, would you be lukewarm?
the sun, would you be burnt?
music, would you be tone-deaf?
a battery, would you be energized?
a time clock, would you be late?
a circus, would you be the clown?
jewelry, would you be a cubic zircon?
a sport, would you be the MVP?
milk, would you be cottage cheese?
a party, would you stay all night?
toothpaste, would you be a cavity?
a riddle, would you get the punch line?
school, would you be illiterate?
a baby, would you be potty trained?
a mouse, would you be a trap?
easy, would you succeed?
difficult, would you say yes to His will?

CHAPTER TWO

FOOD FOR THOUGHT

IN HIS WORD

Jesus said in His word that He would work it out,
so what are you fretting and worried about?
He said in His book to give your issues to Him.
Cast all of your cares and do not worry about them.
The bible states that He really loves you,
so much that He died and rose again too.
Jesus said in His holy word that vengeance is Mine.
If you let Him handle it, your situation will work out fine.
It is written that He desires the praise.
He wants the honor and glory in different ways.
It says in His word that there will be no gods before Him.
If you put people or possessions first, He will remove them.
Several passages command us to love one another,
that includes your neighbors, enemies, sisters and brothers.
The word emphasizes that through Him all things can be done.
All of your fights and battles are already won.
It is written that He cannot tell a lie.
Everything that He says is going to fly.
The word also points out that He never fails.
He is still in control when the storms of life prevail.
You can look it up and read that He is coming again.
He did not tell us where or when.
Jesus said in His word that He is coming back for His own.
He is not going to call and warn us on the telephone.
You need to get your relationship right.
He is coming back like a thief in the night.
All you have to do is confess and believe.
Ask yourself if you will be ready to leave.

SITUATIONS

Sometimes things happen unexpectedly
and cause us to fall down on bended knees.
We do not understand what has taken place
and it feels like we might fall flat on our face.
Situations happen suddenly; life changes very fast.
We do not know how long our tests will last.
We just have to accept it and go along with the facts.
We dust ourselves off and get right back on track.
Events happen and cause us to look around.
The news that we received knocked us on the ground.
Situations happen to make us strong
and we need to realize that the trials will not last long.
Things happen and cause us to change our ways.
For everything that we do, there is a price to pay.
God allows events to happen to take us to another level,
even though we still have to deal with the devil.
Sometimes things happen because a blessing is on the way
and this is the preparation for a better day.
Life shakes us up because God has something to say.
He wants our undivided attention so He allowed it that way.
We have to give it over and trust Him to work it out.
It does not matter if we don't understand what it's all about.
We have to be still and listen for His voice.
If we are backed up in a corner, we do not have much choice.
We have to surrender and finally let go
and have a talk with Jesus because He already knows.
When situations occur and we do not know what to do,
remember that the bible states that God loves you.
God is in control and He is always thinking about you.
Let Him fight your battles because that is what He wants to do.
Tell Him about your concerns and let Him heal your pain.
Do not handle it on your own because you could go insane.
Give Him your worries; let Him have all of them.
He loves you very much; cast your cares on Him.
There is nothing too hard for God because He can handle anything.
Let Him work it out and enjoy the peace that surrendering will bring.

GIVE UP YOUR STASH

In order for you to have a clear mind,
you have to give up your stash.
There is no way that you can focus
if you continue to hold on to your trash.
You cannot give some of your issues over
and keep your main concern from Him.
Surrendering is about giving up everything,
each and every one of them.
It is the one thing that you are holding on to
that is doing all of the messing.
The issue that you are keeping from Him
might be in the way of your next blessing.
God knows what is best so give it to Him
and stop trying to be the one in control.
Your stash is causing you too much pain,
why don't you let it go?
Do not carry the weight around any longer,
you can surrender your concerns today.
Now is the best time
for you to give your stash away.

HAVE YOU EVER

Have you ever thought you needed a quick fix?
Have you seen Him show up while in the mix?
Have you ever had to dodge, hide, or creep?
Have you been told that God's love is deep?
Have you ever wanted something that did not belong to you?
Have you heard God say that His love is true?
Have you ever cherished something that was not Jesus?
Have you heard Him say that He is the only one who can please us?
Have you ever been caught up and blocked the whole world out?
Have you heard Jesus say that is what forgiveness is about?
Have you ever been out of line and in the wrong position?
Have you heard Him tell you to be still and listen?
Have you ever held on to something and did not want to give it over?
Have you heard Jesus say that He wants to be your lover?
Have you ever asked the question, "Do you really love me"?
Have you heard Jesus say that your answer is at Calvary?

CHAPTER THREE

ON THE DIRECT LINE TO JESUS

GIVE ME A CLEAN HEART

I need You to clean up my heart
and I will be able to have a new start.
I need You to clean up my talk
and that will help me with my walk.
I need You to clean up my friends
because I do not want them to be found in sin.
I want You to clean up my house
so that You can step in and be my spouse.
I need You to clean up my feet and hands
so that I will be able to take a stand.
I need You to clean up my life
and I will commit and be Your wife.
I need You to clean up my family
because I want them to know You like You know me.
I want You to clean up my ears
and I will not get caught up in everything that I hear.
I want You to clean up my eyes
so that Satan's attacks will not come as a surprise.
I want You to clean me up right now.
You are the one who can do it and You know how.
I want to be pure and holy for You
so that I can do the work that You called me to do.
Clean me up and make me brand new
so that when people look at me, they will be able to see You.

YOU PROMISED ME

You promised to never leave me and I can truly say
that You have never left me alone, not even for one day.
You promised to stay right by my side.
You were even there when I tried to hide.
You promised to take care of me.
You stood by Your word when I could not see.
You promised to supply my every need.
You stood on this promise and showed up indeed.
You promised to watch me during the night.
When the storms of life were raging, I was not out of Your sight.
You promised to protect me during the day.
You charged Your angels to guard me and kept the enemy at bay.
You promised to give me my daily bread.
Not only did You sustain me, but my family You fed.
You promised that You would always love me.
You showed me that real love was shown at Calvary.
You promised that You are coming back for me.
You prepared a special place in Heaven and that is where I will be.
Thank you for being so good to me.
Thank you for being faithful and for grace and mercy.

A LETTER TO JESUS

I am asking You to forgive me
for not trusting Your word that I can clearly see.
You told me to surrender and give it to You
and watch You handle it the way that You do.
I am coming to You as humbly as I know how.
I surrender my concerns and worries right now.
I give them to You so that I can do Your will.
I put my trust in You and I am going to be still.
I will close my mouth and listen to You speak.
I am waiting on You and in Your word I seek.
The victory is already won; I just have to go through.
I will not go alone because I am going with You.
I know that You will show up and have Your way.
I expect a blessing from You today.
I am thanking You in advance for what You are going to do.
I know without a doubt that Your promises are true.
Thank you for providing for me and meeting me at my need.
Thank you for being a keeper, indeed.
Thank you for Your voice and making sure that I hear it.
Thank you for the aid of the Holy Spirit.
Thank you for doing what You said You would.
Thank you Lord for being so good.

DOING MINISTRY

Thank you Lord for choosing me out of everyone that You know.
There is something that You want me to do; the bible tells me so.
You have a special assignment and that is why You chose me.
No one else can do it and that is how You designed it to be.
The experiences that I have gone through, even though I did not see,
were meant for good and not evil so that I could do ministry.
I did not understand why I went through so much pain.
I understand now that it was for someone else to gain.
There were times when I suffered from guilt and shame.
I did things I said I would never do and I played dangerous games.
The Lord brought me out and said that was enough.
My life has not been easy and the road has been rough.
I went through the drama for a particular reason.
The Lord has work for me to do and this is my season.
I am willing and available to help somebody out
because that is what my calling and ministry is about.
You could have picked anyone but I thank You for choosing me.
My shackles have been lifted so that I can do ministry.
Use me Lord to do whatever You will.
I know without a doubt that deliverance is real.

YES LORD

Lord, what is it that You want to do with me?
Open my eyes so that I can clearly see.
What is it that You would have me to do?
How do you want me to serve and work for You?
I know that everything that I have gone through
is because there is something that You want me to do.
My story that I have been afraid to tell
could save someone from experiencing a burning hell.
I know that You are shaping and cleaning me too
because of the ministry that You have called me to do.
I know that You are preparing something for me
because You are shaking and stirring me.
You are making me whole and putting me in position.
You have specifically told me to be still and listen.
If I heed to Your voice and wait on You,
You promised that You would tell me what to do.
The work is already done and scheduled in Your word.
Faith cometh by hearing, which is what I heard.
All I have to do is submit to Your will
and let You have Your way regardless of how I feel.
I have fought long enough and tried it my way.
I am tired of fighting so I surrender today.
Everything that I have experienced will work out for my good.
Go ahead and use me like You said You would.
I am willing to be a voice and a vessel for You.
Tell me what You want me to do.
I promise that I will take this opportunity
to do Your will and give You the glory.
This is not about me or how I feel.
Today I surrender and say yes to Your will.

CHAPTER FOUR

TRIBUTES TO LOVED ONES

MOM AND DAD

God has blessed you to see one more year.
Is it hard to believe that another anniversary is here?
In spite of everything that you are going through,
The Lord has something for both of you to do.
I do not know what it is; He is the only one who knows.
He continues to allow your blessings to flow.
Dad, I hope and pray that you realize
that God has blessed you with a precious prize.
A faithful woman who sticks by your side,
I hope that you acknowledge her as your pride.
A loyal woman who stands by you,
in times like these, that is hard to do.
A godly woman who lifts you up in prayer,
she keeps holding on because God is there.
A beautiful woman who has honored her vows,
in sickness and in health, she says hallelujah anyhow.
I hope you realize the gift that God has given you.
Love and cherish her because her commitment is true.
Mom, I hope you thank God for your ministry.
You are going through this process for others to see.
God is using you in a special way.
It is because of grace and mercy that you are here today.
When you get weary and your days seem long,
continue to call on Jesus and He will make you strong.
When you take care of Dad by doing all that you do,
not only are you serving him but you are serving the Lord too.
Thank you Lord for the stormy weather.
Thank you Lord that they are still together.
Give them the strength to make it through the day.
Thank you Lord for making a way.

MOM

P is for PATIENCE for dealing with me.
A is for ALWAYS being the best you can be.
T is for TRUTHFUL, that is how you are.
R is for READILY available, no matter near or far.
I is for INDEPENDENCE, which is what you teach.
C is for CARING in everything that you preach.
I is for IMPORTANT, I could not make it without you.
A is for AUTHENTIC in all the things you do.

L is for LOVE, you have so much to give out.
O is for OPAL, you are a jewel, no doubt.
U is for UNDERSTANDING, your heart is so dear.
I is for INCOMPLETE, that is what I would be if you were not here.
S is for SWEET, you are much sweeter than honey.
E is for EXHILERATE, your disposition is so sunny.

M is for MIGHTY, you are very strong.
C is for CHRISTIAN, you know to whom you belong.
C is for CLASSIC, you are one of a kind.
A is for ACCURATE, you have a deep mind.
B is for BEAUTY, you are very pretty.
E is for EVERYTHING, you mean the world to me.

A NOTE FOR MY DAD

Looking back on my childhood and the experiences that I had,
I was never proud to call you my dad.
I did not like to be around you because I was afraid of you.
I hated the things that you used to do.
It was not until I left home that I realized
that you were capable of being a dad and that came as a surprise.
When you told me that you loved me and you were not drinking
caused me to do some serious thinking.
The main reason that I changed my perception of you
was because you did not handle your problems like you used to.
When you were mad, you no longer slammed doors and walked out.
You communicated with us and did not yell and shout.
When you were upset, you no longer stayed out all night.
I guess you finally realized that was not right.
When something was on your mind, you no longer took it out on us.
We did not make any progress when we would argue and fuss.
You finally put those old behaviors behind
and that proved to me that you could be loving and kind.
Life is better now that things are not like they used to be.
I am grateful that you are a part of our family.
I am glad that time has taken its course.
I am thankful that you and Mom did not get a divorce.
I know that life has not been easy and the road has been rough.
With God's help, we made it through times that were tough.
I do not want this day to pass without letting you know
how I feel about you now and have the opportunity to show.
I love you and need you in a special way.
I hope that you enjoy your Father's Day.

HAPPY BIRTHDAY DAD

I thank God for allowing you to see another year.
Satan tried to take you out but the Lord kept you here.
There are a few things that I want to say
as you continue to celebrate life on your birthday.
God has been good and has blessed your life,
in spite of all of your sickness and strife.
The road has not been easy but you remained strong.
I am thankful that tribulations do not last very long.
Life is only temporary on this side.
Set your sights on Heaven because that is where you will abide.
There will be no more diabetes, cancer, neuropathy, or pain.
There will be a whole lot of blessings and peace to gain.
In spite of everything that you have been through,
the Lord is still blessing and watching over you.
He deserves all of the praise, honor, and glory.
He wants you to bless someone by telling your story.
Keep in mind during this holiday season
that God healed your body and kept you alive for a reason.
Christmas is not about presents, Santa Claus, or Christmas trees.
Jesus Christ and His love are greater than these.
On your birthday, Christmas, and New Year's Day,
be thankful that God continues to make a way.
If you think birthdays and holidays should be filled with gifts,
just look in the mirror and your spirits should lift.

HAPPY BIRTHDAY SIS

On your special day, I do not want to miss,
the opportunity to send wishes to my big sis.
I am excited about what the Lord is doing in your life,
in spite of the hard times and misery and strife.
He has scheduled your days; the word says this is true.
The Lord has an assignment for you to do.
He has purposed this ministry especially for you.
There is something unique that He wants you to do.
I do not know what it is but He can tell you.
He will make it plain and clear and will see you through.
You have to surrender your will and your way.
You must listen to everything that He has to say.
You have to give up your power and control.
You no longer have an agenda and cannot be the hero.
You have to give up the things that have you bound.
Once you surrender, your life will turn around.
You have to be still and listen for Him to speak.
You need to be prayerful and in His word you must seek.
He wants your mind, body, and soul.
You have to stop fighting and completely let go.
He has so much in store and it is especially for you.
You have to surrender and do what He wants you to do.
It is because of grace and mercy that you made it another year.
Keep holding on because your breakthrough is near.

ESPECIALLY FOR THE BRIDE

I know that you are elated on your special day.
I will not let it pass without a couple of things to say.
First of all, I can recall when you were just a pup.
Today I look at you and you are all grown up.
I remember the first day that you came home.
LaVonnda and I went to KC so that you could be alone.
When we returned, I did not know there would be so much to do,
while helping Mom and Dad take care of you.
I remember the day when you were only one,
you were diagnosed with diabetes and the family became undone.
But we had a strong mother and a loving God,
on the road to diabetes, our family began to trod.
Time went on and it became a daily routine,
to check your blood, give you a shot, and have a snack in between.
Diabetes did not affect your ability to play
because that is what we did each and every day.
More time passed and it was embedded in me
that it was my responsibility to take care of Little Nellie.
I did it with all of my heart and I did it with pride.
A closeness and friendship developed inside.
We shared the same room; we bonded in our sleep.
The relationship that we had was extremely deep.
I did not want anything bad to happen to you.
I did everything in my power to keep you safe too.
At school, the movies, at play, and even the mall,
I made sure that I would protect you from them all.
No matter where we went, Mom and Dad would say to me,
"Make sure that you watch out for Little Nellie".
The bond that we shared became even deeper.
You were my little baby and I was your keeper.
Not only was I your bodyguard but you looked out for me too.
Because of your devotion, I will always be grateful to you.
One incident that sticks out in my head
is the day that you rescued me because I could have ended up dead.
I thank God for using you in my life that day.
Ever since then I looked at you in a different way.

The meaning of sister was genuine and true.
From that day on, I had a new respect for you.
When I went to college, I did not want to say good-bye.
I was afraid that our relationship might die.
But we talked and wrote and time seemed much longer.
The distance seemed to make our relationship stronger.
It was your turn to decide where you wanted to go to school.
You came to college with me and I thought it was cool.
I was glad that we were living in the same town.
We grew even closer because you were two doors down.
We had our ups and downs but we were always there.
I never imagined the bond that sisters could share.
We partied, we chilled out, we laughed, and we cried.
We made it through because of the love inside.
Our bond was so strong that you were tattooed in my heart.
Our invisible pact stated that we would never part.
Then in June of 94, you took a job in KC.
I was sad and depressed because you were leaving me.
I did not know what my role was supposed to be
because I did not think that you could survive without me.
The miles did not separate us; we still spent quality time.
Either I was at your house or you were at mine.
I hated to leave you and could not wait until we were together again.
Not only were you my little sissy, you were my best friend.
Then Marlon came along and entered your life.
I did not see anything except misery and strife.
I did not want him to take you from me.
I was your big sissy and you were my little baby.
I tried everything in my power that I knew to be mean.
I wanted him out of your life; I wanted him out of the scene.
It was not him personally; it was the way that I felt.
The thought of losing you would make my heart melt.
We talked about him many times and I knew he was important to you.
You wanted me to accept him because your love for him was true.
I should have told you what was really going on
because the whole time you thought that I did not like Marlon.
Three years went by and I knew that I was not going to win.
I decided to accept him, bear it, and grin.

35

I am going to do something so that we both can continue to grow.
I have decided that today I am going to let you go.
I will not look at you as my little baby but for the woman that you are.
Because of God's grace, you have come so far.
I will continue to look at you as my best friend.
We will be close until the end.
I am turning you over to God to let Him have His way.
I wish you all of the happiness on your wedding day.
Always remember that our friendship is true.
Always remember that I really love you.

MY BEST FRIEND

Whenever you think that no one cares,
I want to assure you that I am always right there.
Whenever you are overwhelmed and want to run and hide,
just remember that I am by your side.
In spite of how intense our lives have been,
I am grateful that you are my best friend.
I am blessed to share my life with someone as special as you.
Our friendship is deep and the bond that we share is true.
I cherish each moment and treasure every memory.
I am thankful for the time that you have spent with me.
I know in my heart that you truly care.
Regardless of the situations, you have always been there.
As far as friendship goes, you have passed the test.
I want you to know that your friendship is the best.

PASTOR

I have this all worked out so what are you worrying for?
I am the One who gave you the vision and you are in a war.
All you need to do is surrender everything to Me.
I will handle the situation and you will be present to see.
This assignment is bigger than you but I am in control.
I knew that you could not handle it so you must let it go.
I am going to use you as My vessel so that My will is carried out.
The victory is yours so what are you overwhelmed about?
Do not pace the floor or stay up all night.
Do not worry about a thing; this battle is not yours to fight.
I promised in My word that I would never leave nor forsake you.
I know what is going on and this is what I called you to do.
I want you to be still and listen for Me to speak.
Pray without ceasing and in My word you must seek.
I have given Satan permission to do what he wants to do.
I made it perfectly clear that he could not take your life from you.
No matter how hectic your day turns out to be,
you need to spend some intimate time with Me.
You are safe in My arms and nothing will stand in your way.
You must give Me complete control and surrender today.
Go ahead and praise Me for what I am going to do.
Be ready at all times because I am going to use you.

DEL

Do you know that this is a set up for you?
God is getting ready to show you that His promises are true.
The events that are happening in your life today,
is a result of you letting the Lord have His way.
He checked the situation out and He knows what is going on.
He has taken care of everything because you are His son.
Nothing is too hard for Him to handle or fix.
He is in control even when you are in the mix.
God can work it out when you give up your control.
He wants you to surrender your mind, body, and soul.
Cast all of your cares on Him and do not worry about a thing.
Seek Him first and enjoy the peace that He brings.
God did not give you the spirit of fear.
Tell Him your concerns and know that He is near.
The battle is already won; your situation is worked out.
He wants to hear from you because that is what prayer is about.
I can testify that God is not intimidated by cancer.
That is one of the reasons that I became a dancer.
I am a witness that God has a plan for your family.
There is a blessing in this storm, you just watch and see.
The trials that you are going through will not last very long.
Your faith becomes tested and you become strong.
Do not try to handle this situation in your own way.
Give it over to Jesus and let Him have His way.
I love you and you are constantly in my prayers.
Continue to seek God first because He is the One who really cares.

CARM

Do you know what is happening to you today?
God wants your attention because He has something to say.
Be still and trust Him and listen for His voice.
At this particular time, you do not have much choice.
God has an assignment that He wants you to do.
He allowed you to lie down so that His instructions come through.
Many lives will be touched and He is going to use you.
There is a special work that only you can do.
This day was scheduled a long time ago.
It was recorded in His book because the bible tells me so.
Count it all joy and let Him have His way.
This is a set up for a better day.
He is preparing you for the work that He wants done.
In order to get it accomplished, He said that you are the one.
In order to complete it, He has to work some things out of you.
He is fixing you up and making you brand new.
He loves you but He is not going to let you stay the same.
You will not leave this place the same way that you came.
In your quiet time, remember that God is right there.
He reminded you in His word to cast all of your cares.
Use this time wisely and get some rest.
You will not be in this situation long because this is only a test.
I love you and I am lifting up your name in prayer.
Seek God first because He is the One who really cares.
You are in the hands of the Doctor who handles everything.
Keep your focus on Jesus and watch the healing that it brings.

NIQUE

I was just sitting here
thinking about you.
I have alot on my mind
and many things to do.
I want you to know
that you are important to me.
I am grateful for being a part of your life
and for this ministry.
Thank you for caring enough
to confide in me.
I do not take it for granted
because I know how women can be.
I am excited about the Lord
and what He has planned for us.
In spite of all of the critics
and the headaches and the fuss.
God has placed us together
for a particular reason.
He has some work for us to do
and this is our season.
I want you to know
that I am proud to work with you.
I am excited about our friendship
because I care about you.
I want you to know
that you are special to me.
I will continually pray
for God to bless our ministry.

LaShawn D. Childs

AUNTIE

There is not a day that goes by
that you are not in my prayers.
God knows what you are going through
and He is always right there.
Sometimes things happen in our lives
and we do not understand them.
He wants you to surrender your cares
and lean on Him.
He never puts more on you than you can bear
and He knows how much you can take.
He wants you to try Him at His word
and discover that His love is not fake.
Keep on fighting the good fight
and your pain will not last very long.
Put your hand in the Master's hand
and He will make you strong.
I am praying for you
so that you will be able to stand the test.
Everything that you are going through is a set up
so that you can be blessed.
I want you to know that I am here
and you have a special place in my heart.
Cast all of your cares on Him
and that is where your healing will start.

SISTER JAMES

I want to let you know
that you have touched my life in a special way.
I want to share a thought with you
on your special day.
The first time that I heard you preach,
I knew that you were chosen by God.
I knew that He was using you
because what you shared made me feel odd.
Who in the world told this little woman
about events that happened in my life?
Who told this total stranger about me
and my pain, abuse, and strife?
I knew that it was only Him
because I had not shared any of that stuff.
The Lord used you to encourage me
and He used very tough.
I cannot tell you how many times
your name has come out of my lips.
Even when you were not the topic of conversation,
sometimes your name would slip.
As I mature in the faith,
my prayer is that people will see Jesus in me.
I want my light to shine
and be as beautiful as I can be.
My prayer is that God will continue to use you
and that you let Him have His way.
May God richly bless you
on your special day.

LaShawn D. Childs

GRAM

This is not an easy task for me
because this was the world's greatest grandma, you see.
She was the most precious mother and loved one too.
In order for me to heal, this is what I need to do.
Words cannot do justice of how I feel
but I can definitely say that her love was real.
It started way back, a long time ago,
I knew back then that she loved us so.
I saw her everyday because she was only two doors down.
My grandma was the best babysitter around.
She usually had something baked for us
and I never heard her put up a fuss.
She would usually send us to the store.
She wanted cigarettes so that is what we would go for.
She trusted us to go because the store was not very far.
She would give us some change to get a Mr. Goodbar.
Whenever we wanted to, she would let us spend the night.
She would tuck us and say, "Don't let the bed bugs bite".
Most of the time, we would go over her house to play.
On several occasions, she made homemade clay.
It was not until I got older that I really knew
that my love for Gram was genuine and true.
Time went by and she moved to the other side of town.
On special occasions, she would come around.
When I called her on the phone, she would always yell,
"You'll have to speak louder, is this LaShawn or LaNelle?"
When I asked what she doing, I can hear her say,
"Oh, I'm just sitting here working on my crochet".
I thought about her often and I called just to say hi.
She said if I was going out that she wanted me to drop by.
If days had passed since she seen me, she would say that
it sure looked like I was getting fat.
Gram had a personality that was very caring.
If it was her last, she was always sharing.
She would give up her money and belongings too,
even though none of her clothes would fit you.

Her money was limited but she did not care.
No matter what the cost, she would be there.
Her heart was so big that you could not help but adore.
To everyone around, her love she would pour.
Her mind was stayed on Jesus; He was the head of her life.
She never doubted Him in all of her pain and strife.
Out of her mouth, she talked the Christian talk.
In all things she did, she walked the Christian walk.
She trusted in the Lord for so long
and He is the reason that our family remained strong.
Speaking of family, she cherished hers so,
even when Grandpa decided to go.
Of course, that situation turned out wrong
but she stood by her children and the Lord kept her strong.
She took care of business and got her kids out
because that is what being a real mama is about.
As time went on, she started to complain
that her knees and legs were full of pain.
Her eyes started bothering her and as a matter of fact,
later she developed cataracts.
In spite of her pain, she kept on pushing,
sitting in her chair on her homemade cushion.
She sat like a chipmunk holding gum in her cheeks.
She chewed the same pieces for several weeks.
The sun bothered her eyes so she tried to hide from the light.
She wore sunglasses during the day and at night.
I could go on and on because I knew her so well.
I am telling you that my Gram was swell.
She has finally gone on to a better day
and God has taken her pain away.
She is in a place where a new day has sprung.
She will never have to worry about a clogged lung.
She will never experience any more pain, you see.
She will not complain about another stiff knee.
The Lord promised to rid her of hardened arteries.
She is no longer dealing with shut-off kidneys.
She resides in a place where she has her own spot.
She will never experience another blood clot.

LaShawn D. Childs

My grandma is in Heaven and she is free to roam.
She did not have to go to a nursing home.
She lives in a place where she has it made.
She will never wear another hearing aid.
There will be no more doctors so she won't have to fight us
because her body is free from arthritis.
She will never have to deal with astigmatism
and her stomach is free from that aneurysm.
She resides in a place where health comes in masses.
You are healed Grandma so take off your sunglasses.
Family, do not fret because Gram is well.
She is safe in Heaven and that is where she will dwell.
Even though from this place she is physically gone,
her love and her spirit will forever live on.

GRANDMA

Here we are, during this time of the year,
Thanksgiving dinner is served and you are not here.
Why did you leave me all alone?
I am mad because you cannot answer your telephone.
I rode by your house and could not stop.
You were not in there and my tears began to drop.
I have never felt so much pain.
Sometimes it feels like I am going insane.
Did you know that I graduated college in May?
You were the only person missing on my special day.
I wish that you could have been cheering in the crowd.
I know that you would have been proud.
I wish that you could come and see my new place.
I would love to see the expression on your face.
I know that you would make an afghan for my loveseat.
It would make my house look nice and neat.
You would ask a million questions about my job and what I do.
I would answer all of them because I want to talk to you.
Did you know that I bought a new car?
I wish you could ride in it and we would go far.
We would ride until I filled you in on the latest news.
We would go as far as you would like; I would let you choose.
Did you know that my boyfriend is no longer with me?
I guess that relationship was not meant to be.
You knew that our relationship was not going to work all along
because the first time you met him you said that we did not belong.
Did you know that your picture is on my nightstand?
It is the one of you holding your face in your hand.
When I wake up in the morning, you are the first person that I see.
I wish that you were here so that you could see me.
Did you know that there is not a day that goes by
that I get so angry and want to cry?
I am mad because you left me and moved away.
I am mad because you are not here on another Thanksgiving day.
Why did you leave me here with so much pain?
Do you think I will be able to see you again?

47

CHAPTER FIVE

HEARING HIM LOUD AND CLEAR

BE STILL AND KNOW THAT I AM GOD

In order for you to understand My will,
the first thing you need to do is be still.
Close your mouth and listen to Me.
I know what is best and how things should be.
Give up your will and let go of your power and control.
Relinquish it to Me because I already know.
Let Me have the issues that have you bound.
Surrender your concerns that have you running around.
Stop trying to figure everything out
because that is not what surrendering is about.
You do not have to know all of the details.
When you try to fix it, you will probably fail.
Study My word and hide it in your heart.
When you accept Me, our relationship will start.
Put into action My word that you hear.
Always be confident that I am near.
Trust and believe that I know what is best.
Be ready to stand and go through the test.
I promised to supply all of your needs.
I will step in on time and will make a way indeed.
Stop trying to fight it and let Me have My way.
Tomorrow is not promised so surrender today.
If during this process you start to feel odd,
be still and know that I am God.

LET ME HAVE IT

Whatever your situation is, turn it over to Me.
I will not tolerate you serving two masters, you see.
Let Me have it and I will work it out.
You do not have time to sit around and pout.
Give it over to Me because it does not belong to you.
You can start loving Me like you are supposed to.
The situation that you are in has caused you too much pain.
There were times when you thought you were going insane.
In your life, I want to be first.
When you try My living water, you will never thirst.
Let Me have it, it will not cost you a dime.
I am available to you all of the time.
Let Me have it, I will not make you sick.
I will never let you down; I am the best of the pick.
Let Me have it, I will never break down,
I will not leave you stranded or running around.
Let Me have it, I can stay all night,
You will not get tired of Me and we will not fight.
I can supply your every need.
When you get hungry, I can always feed.
My love for you is very deep.
With this type of love, you will never have to creep.
There is no doubt that I can take care of you, Honey.
Do not worry about a thing because I own all of the money.
Have faith in Me because I know what is best.
I am better than any of the rest.
Surrender your situation because it does not belong to you.
Give it over to Me and I will show you what is true.
Whatever you are searching for, I can give you today.
You must surrender everything and let Me have My way.

WHY ARE YOU RUNNING

When was the last time you stopped and sat down?
Why have you been running all around?
What are you trying to keep out of your head?
Why are you focusing on other things instead?
Why are you constantly on the go?
What is it that you do not want others to know?
When was the last time you took a long nap?
When was the last time you sat in My lap?
Why are you trying to keep yourself busy?
Do you really think you can run from Me?
No matter where you go, I am already there.
No matter what you do, I really do care.
You can run but you cannot hide from Me.
You are not smart enough and you never will be.
This situation is causing you too much tension.
You know, the issue that you do not want to mention.
I have it worked out and the victory is already won.
Save yourself some energy and stop trying to run.
I am going to have My way regardless of what you say or do.
I said it in My word and you know that it is true.
There is nothing that you can do to stop what I have planned.
The enemy cannot even stop it because he has already been banned.
Slow yourself down and just be still.
You are making things worse because you are out of My will.
Give this situation to Me while you have the choice.
Open up My word and listen for My voice.
The things that I have planned for you are already done.
Surrender yourself and stop trying to run.

LaShawn D. Childs

HOW MANY TIMES

How many times do I have to tell you
that your body does not belong to you?
I paid for it on Calvary
and there are a couple of things you cannot do.
How many times do I have to tell you
that you need to learn how to dress?
Those tight shorts, jeans, and mini-skirts
really look a mess.
How many times do I have to tell you
that it is a sin to fornicate?
People usually obey this command
after it is too late.
If fornicate is over your head,
I will say that single people cannot have sex.
Why do you keep holding on to
and hooking up with your ex?
How many times do I have to tell you
that it usually starts off with a hug?
Before you know it,
you graduate to a kiss, squeeze, or a tug.
How many times do I have to tell you
that you cannot have sex until you say, "I do"?
If you waited until you were married,
you would not be going through.
How many times do I have to tell you
to keep lustful thoughts out of your mind?
Eventually you will try to justify
by doing a little bump and grind.
How many times do I have to tell you
to stop testing yourself to see if you are strong?
As weak and vulnerable as the flesh is,
you know that it does not take very long.
How many times do I have to tell you
that there is no temptation that you cannot bear?
Stop trying to handle it your own strength
and use Me because I am always there.

How many times do I have to tell you
that I know what is best for you?
You need to be patient and wait on Me
and trust what I can do.
How many times do I have to tell you
that I have someone especially for you?
I am cleaning and fixing that person up
just like I am preparing you too.
How many of you will not be ready
because you are found on your back?
In order for Me to get you ready,
you have to stay out of the sack.
Stop acting like you are married
and wait until you are wed.
In the meantime, wait on Me
and keep yourself out of the bed.
How many times do I have to tell you?
I have told you more than thrice.
Your body is My holy temple
so present it as a living sacrifice.

CHAPTER SIX

INSTRUCTIONS
ABOUT RELATIONSHIPS

MY SISTER'S KEEPER

I do not understand it and it sure is a shame
that we cannot call each other by name.
We do not want anybody to introduce us
because it is too much hassle and too much fuss.
I don't need a woman to be my friend
because I get along much better with men.
Women gossip too much and become too sticky.
When it comes to my circle, I am very picky.
Women are possessive and will often trip.
If you talk to somebody else, your friend will flip.
You were my friend first and I don't want to share,
but do what you want to because I don't really care.
You better believe that I am not trusting a female again.
I have been hurt by a woman who said I was her friend.
Look at that girl; she thinks she's all that.
I don't know who lied to her but that girl is too fat.
She has on too much make-up and her clothes are too tight.
She lies and is two-faced and she knows she aint right.
That is not her real hair and she bought those nails.
She has a couple of boyfriends and they both are in jail.
She has slept with every man who lives in this town.
It does not matter who they are; she has been messing around.
She drinks all of the time and she probably smokes crack.
You better watch out because she will stab you in the back.
She has all of those kids and they really are a bother.
Every single one of them has a different father.
The man that lives with her is unemployed and she does not care.
She would rather stay in the system collecting welfare.
She tries to justify her lifestyle due to the pain of her past.
Come on Girlfriend, how long will that same excuse last?
Don't you know that there are many women hurting today?
Every woman expresses hurt in her own unique way.
Instead of being standoffish, why not find out her name?
You will probably find out that she is in pain.
Instead of being judgmental, take that woman in
and find out if she has ever had a true friend.

Instead of spreading her business and talking a bunch,
extend the invitation to take her to lunch.
Instead of running from her, another thing you can do,
take that woman shopping with you.
Instead of being hateful and wearing that frown,
speak to her and let your guard down.
Don't look at her clothes but look at her heart.
You would be amazed at the bond that could start.
Instead of being jealous, compliment and praise her.
Don't be mad at her because she is confident and sure.
Look past her actions and look at her life.
You can probably relate to her confusion and strife.
When you dig deeper, you will find that the problem is not her.
You have your own unresolved issues and pain, for sure.
It could be your insecurities and your self-esteem
that keeps that woman from being on your team.
The sister that you are running from
could be the one that God uses for your deliverance to come.
Today is the day to break off those chains.
Stop mistreating her and deal with your pain.
Embrace and love her and pray for her too.
The woman that you are running from is really you.
Take off your mask and expose the real you.
Let God use your sister to help bring you through.

GO AND GET YOUR FRIEND

Why is it so hard to let someone back in,
when you have been hurt by someone you called your friend?
You refuse to hang out and do not want to sup.
You think it is safer to put your guard up.
Don't say that you forgive you when that is not what you mean.
You make it a point to never forget the scene.
Why do you cut innocent people off because of the pain you feel?
You think your mind is confused and you do not know what is real.
You think keeping your distance makes everything all right.
The resentment that you feel makes you want to fight.
Why is it hard to leave mistakes in the past?
As long as you are the victim, you think you have control at last.
Accept the fact that you will have good and bad days.
In order to move on, you have to get rid of your evil ways.
Why not seek the Lord and ask Him to heal your pain?
If you do not close this chapter, you could possibly go insane.
In your particular situation, what would Jesus do?
Try to imagine where you would be if He had not forgiven you.
Stop apologizing over and over for the same sin.
Brush yourself off and go and get your friend.
Renew your commitment and wipe the slate clean.
Stop being guarded, defensive, and mean.
Ask God to be in the middle of your relationship.
Stop wasting time and get on with your fellowship.
Life is too short and time is going by too fast.
Quit harping over mistakes that were made in the past.
Take the first step and get back on track.
Go and get your friend back.

LaShawn D. Childs

CHECK YOURSELF

If everybody in the church was just like me,
what kind of church would my church be?
If everybody had the same thoughts that I have in my head,
how many people would end up hurt or even dead?
If everybody was as wishy-washy as I can be,
how many people would want to be bothered with me?
If everybody focused on someone else when they were in the wrong,
how many people would stay in the church very long?
If everybody in the church had my heart,
how much trouble and confusion would start?
If everybody covered up to hide all of his or her mess,
how many people would run out to buy a new suit or a dress?
If every woman hid behind her nails and her hair done just right,
then who would know that she cried all through the night?
If every man had to purchase a six-button suit,
would that cover up that he did not feel cute?
If every teenager had to have sex to get some attention,
how many parents would be sent to detention?
If everybody in the church had to sing and shout,
how many people would go home and cuss somebody out?
If everybody smiled to cover up their pain,
how many people would stop acting vain?
If everybody in the church had to purchase the latest car,
how many people would be driving behind scars?
If everybody had to move into a bigger place,
how many people with bad credit would fall on their face?
If everybody in the church tried to keep up with Mr. and Mrs. Jones,
how many people would try to take out more loans?
What do you think would happen if one day,
we would walk in the church and throw all masks away?
What would happen if everybody cut off their hair?
Would that change your mind about what you were going to wear?
What would happen if we all had to ride the bus
and there were not any cars to be jealous of or to put up a fuss?
What would happen if we all lived in a tent
and nobody could brag about a house payment or rent?

What would happen if we all made the same amount of money?
Who could criticize the less fortunate and think it was funny?
What would happen if we all would acknowledge that we sin?
Who would you judge and talk about then?
What would happen if people knew that you were hurt
and you could not cover it up with a dress or a shirt?
What would happen if the church would get real?
How many people would be delivered and heal?
What would happen if the church knew the real you?
Would they still speak and treat you the same way that they do?
Let me tell you what would happen if we were all exposed.
All of those fronts and facades would be disposed.
We would find out that none of us really got it going on.
We are all trying to make it and are barely hanging on.
We would find out that we all have weaknesses and struggles too.
Sometimes we get overwhelmed and we do not know what to do.
We would find out that we are all struggling to live right.
Everyday we are in spiritual warfare and a fight.
We are people portraying something that we are not.
We keep living the lie because we have not got caught.
It is up to you to keep hiding or to be real.
You can fool other people but God knows the real deal.
You can pretend that you are better than but it comes as no surprise
that we were all made from dirt when looking through God's eyes.
If everybody in the church was just like me,
what kind of church would my church be?

LADIES NIGHT OUT

I remember when you told Me
that with women you do not fellowship.
You said that women were too messy
and to befriend them is a trip.
I am telling you that you are going to open up to women
and you will share your story.
As a result of your obedience,
I will get the honor and glory.
You are not going to stay in your little circle
because you do not feel like opening up.
You are going to touch the lives of many women
and together you will fellowship and sup.
There are so many women in the world
who need to be ministered to.
One of the ways that they will be delivered
will come from Me using you.
You think that you are being slick
by playing cards and other games.
It might have started out simple
but someone is going to be healed of her pain.
In your card-playing group of women,
each one of you is checking the other one out.
I am preparing and setting the stage
for deliverance to come about.
When I am ready to step in,
each one of you will take a serious look.
You will count up the time that you spend playing cards
and realize that you should be reading My book.
I know that a bond is being developed
but you just watch and see,
that within your circle of card-playing girls,
I am forming a ministry.
Before this ministry develops,
I am fixing and making things right.
Situations are going to get uncomfortable
and I am going to pull some strings very tight.

I know all of your potential
and you are going to stop playing card games.
I love you just the way that you are
but I am not going to let you stay the same.
In order for you to do the work
that I have called you to do,
I am going to cleanse you and make you whole
so that you can be holy and true.
Don't tell Me that you are not going to hang out with women
because of your concerns and doubts.
I am going to bring all women together for ministry
and you will experience a real ladies night out.

CHAPTER SEVEN

DEVELOPING YOUR OWN
RELATIONSHIP
WITH GOD

SPECIAL NEWS BULLETIN

Have you been shipwrecked on GILLIGAN'S ISLAND and want a RESCUE 911? Have you been living a JOKER'S WILD life on the EDGE OF NIGHT? Are you tired of being bound? If so, I would like to share with you the FACTS OF LIFE. I know that times get rough, AS THE WORLD TURNS and I want to assure you that LIFE GOES ON. You might be experiencing some GROWING PAINS and whining GIMME A BREAK. You might be trying to COPS out by saying LET'S MAKE A DEAL because I am YOUNG AND RESTLESS. If you fall into any of these categories, I would like to point you to the GUIDING LIGHT. If you want to be saved, Jesus Christ is the Way, the Truth, and the Life. Once you accept Him, you no longer will be LOST IN SPACE. If you are CLUELESS about what you should do, all you have to do is say OH GOD, I confess with my mouth that Jesus is Lord and I believe in my heart that God raised Jesus from the dead and you will be saved. You do not have to be SAVED BY THE BELL but by the confession of your faith. This process does not have anything to do with WILL AND GRACE but everything to do with mercy and grace.

Maybe your life has been in JEOPARDY and you have been hurt, abused, mistreated, and a prior slave to sin. If that is you, you will need to check into the GENERAL HOSPITAL. Once you get there, you will be referred to the ER. After checking your vital signs, the DOCTORS will tell you that you need A MAKEOVER STORY. This operation is required because you will need to make a change ON THE INSIDE. I know that you are probably wondering how much this surgery is going to cost and I can tell you that the PRICE IS RIGHT. You don't have to worry about the co-pay because the DEBT has already been paid. You will not be given a copy of the bill because the BURDEN OF PROOF is at Calvary. Do not stress yourself about coming up with MO' MONEY because salvation is free. Jesus paid the bill a long time ago. He paid the bill in full on a FRIDAY and I don't think that it was on FRIDAY THE 13TH. On that particular day, He hung, bled, and died for our sins. He stayed in the grave all night Friday. He was there all day Saturday and even SATURDAY NIGHT LIVE. But early Sunday morning, He got up and it was SHOWTIME AT THE APOLLO. No, I was not there, but I can imagine Him saying GOOD MORNING AMERICA, I've got all power in My hands.

Prior to your dismissal from the hospital, you will be instructed to take your NEW BIRTH experience ONE DAY AT A TIME and STEP BY STEP. You will want to take QUANTUM LEAPS but the DOCTORS have advised you to be patient. In order for you to completely heal after your surgery, I am going to give you the INSIDE EDITION. Everything that you need for a complete recovery can be found in your prescription. In His holy word, He says by His stripes you are healed. All you have to do is take a CLOSER LOOK at His book and follow His commands. Time is running out so you need to confess right now. If you are SEARCHING FOR TOMORROW, it might be too late. You are not guaranteed the next 48 HOURS or 60 MINUTES. You do not have to get on the SOUL TRAIN, flag down a TAXI, GET ON THE BUS or even book a flight on an AIRPLANE. Wherever you are, all you have to do is confess and believe and God is faithful and just to FORGIVE AND FORGET your sins and you will be ALL IN THE FAMILY.

I need to tell you that after you accept Jesus, you can expect to be tempted, tested, tried, and attacked by the TERMINATOR. Yes, I am talking about Satan. Some call him a serpent; others call him the devil. He will be very angry because you have turned your back on him and are no longer saying I LOVE LUCY. (That is short for Lucifer) Be sober and vigilant because he is going to send his DUKES OF HAZARD to try and steal, kill, and destroy your life. When they attack, do not panic. God promised to protect and hide you and ALL MY CHILDREN from the enemy even if He has a FULL HOUSE. Do not become discouraged because DOUBLE TROUBLE does not last always. God is not the ARTHUR of confusion. He is all about LAW AND ORDER. The devil cannot do anything without God's permission. You have to trust and believe that FATHER KNOWS BEST. Satan is very busy but God is still in control. Never let your guard down because Satan attacks WITHOUT WARNING. Always be alert and be ready to BAYWATCH, fight, and pray. When Satan comes to attack, look him in his face and call him a LIAR LIAR and fight him with the word of God.

If you are already saved, I would like to encourage those who are LIVING SINGLE. I do not know what your current physical or spiritual condition is but I do know that God wants to get UP CLOSE AND PERSONAL with you. He wants to make a LOVE CONNECTION because He is MAD ABOUT YOU. You do not have to play the DATING GAME because He wants to be number one in your life. For you single women, He wants to be more than your SUPERMAN. He wants to show you what real MIDNIGHT LOVE is. He says that you can come as you are. You do not have to dress a particular way to impress Him so leave your SILK STALKINGS in the drawer. He wants to ROC your world. For those of you who are impatient and are WAITING TO EXHALE, He can give you ENTERTAINMENT TONIGHT and a TONIGHT SHOW. He wants to be your BOSOM BUDDY and ACE VENTURA. He said in His word that you could not serve two masters. He is very jealous and does not want anyone or anything to come before Him. You need to decide WHO'S THE BOSS and remember that CHARLES IS not IN CHARGE. This rule does not have anything to do with L.A. LAW but everything to do with God's law. He can heal you of all of your pain, rejection, and abuse from the past. God is the Potter who is still DESIGNING WOMEN. He is molding and shaping women into BOLD AND BEAUTIFUL jewels that will eventually turn into GOLDEN GIRLS. So, SISTER SISTER, taste and see that the Lord is good and let Him be more than your SIX MILLION DOLLAR MAN. Grab your CANDID CAMERA and take an INTIMATE PORTRAIT with Jesus.

I do not want to forget the single BROTHERS. To all of you MISTER ROGERS who are raising your RUGRATS by yourself, I want to encourage you also. When you are feeling worn out and need someone to talk to, take all of your cares and worries to the MAJOR DAD. He said in His word that the battle is not yours to fight. He will fight it for you. Continue to ask God to bless your LITTLE HOUSE ON THE PRAIRIE and seek God first.

I cannot forget to say something to those who are experiencing the NEWLYWED GAME. I know that it feels wonderful to be on the LOVE BOAT living in FANTASY ISLAND. God knows that FAMILY MATTERS and you are responsible for FAMILY TIES. Even though you are enjoying this moment with your OTHER HALF, God still wants to be first in your marriage.

For those of you who are MARRIED WITH CHILDREN, I would like to encourage you as well. You might be dealing with a PROBLEM CHILD or struggling with BEBE'S KIDS but HONEY DO NOT BLOW UP THE KIDS. Seek God first and watch Him move. They will not be FOREVER YOUNG and one day they will be gone and you will have an EMPTY NEST. If you seek God first, once the kids are gone, you will be able to make some HOME IMPROVEMENTS and become HONEYMOONERS once again.

I would like to share A PERSONAL STORY. I want you to know that I will be getting on the HIGHWAY TO HEAVEN. I am going to the PROMISED LAND where every day is filled with GOOD TIMES and HAPPY DAYS. When I get there, I am going to sing a song that CHARLIES ANGELS will not be able to sing about how I made it over. I do not know when He is coming back but I do know that I will be IN THE HOUSE. ONE FINE DAY, when this life is over, I will mount up with WINGS like eagles and I'll FLY AWAY. I am going to be GONE WITH THE WIND.

Will you be ready? Will you be there? Or will you be like those who did not surrender and are burning IN THE HEAT OF THE NIGHT? Don't be a HARD COPY of those who followed DIFFERENT STROKES. You could end up like GRACE UNDER FIRE and live UNHAPPILY EVER AFTER. She is trying to ESCAPE FROM ALCATRAZ and get to a DIFFERENT WORLD. You better get ready because the KING OF THE HILL is COMING TO AMERICA to make a SUPERMARKET SWEEP and is coming back for His own. We will not have to FACE THE NATION or even JUDGE JUDY but we will MEET THE PRESS and face the FRESH PRINCE of peace. We only have ONE LIFE TO LIVE down here so we better get right so that we can enjoy ANOTHER WORLD.

In conclusion, let me summarize this up by channels. It is as simple as ABC. The wages of CNN is death but the gift of God is eternal life through Jesus Christ. On judgment day, everyone will have to stand before God. He will PREVUE the HISTORY of our lives, even if we have been as sly as a FOX. It does not matter if we have been looking for a quick FX or if we have lived lives that were MTV. Everybody is going to have to give an account of their LIFETIME. God of the USA and the UNIVERSE sent His only Son who was full of TLC to die for us. He paid the price so that we could DISCOVER the way to eternal life. He wants us to become EDUCATED in His word and TOON our hearts and minds over to Him. He died once and for all at Calvary and will not be making an ENCORE performance of that day. He is coming back for His own. I do not know WEATHER it will be today or next week but I do know that it is going to be a TNT experience and you can BET on that.

YOU NEED TO WASH UP

There is nothing that we can do to clean ourselves up from the filthy stains of sin. The bible tells us that while we were yet sinners, Christ died in our place. It is only because of His blood that we are cleansed and made as IVORY as snow. In order for you to become clean, all you have to do is DIAL Him up and tell Him what you want. His line is never too busy so you will never have to worry about hearing that TONE. All you have to do is confess with your mouth that Jesus is Lord and believe in your heart that God raised Jesus from the dead and you will be saved. After you accept Jesus, He promised that He would always be your SAFEGUARD and SHIELD. You do not have to go to the Jordan River or even to the IRISH SPRING. This process takes place in your heart. Wherever you are or whatever you are doing, you can call upon on the name of Jesus and He will CARESS you in His loving arms. It does not matter what you have done in your past. If any man is in Christ, old things have COASTed away and you will have a new LIFEBUOY. Stop JERGENS around and stop wasting time. You need to accept Christ while you have the time. I want to assure you that your new life with Christ will be full of ZEST. He has plans to prosper you and not to harm you. You also need to know that He is coming back one day. He is coming back to get His children. In a twinkling of an eye and with wings like a DOVE, the dead in Christ shall rise. Will you be ready to go?

CHAPTER EIGHT

A FEW WORDS FOR SATAN

DOUBLE FOR MY TROUBLE

You should have took my joy
while you had me down.
You made the mistake of letting me live
and now you are prowling around.
You are not strong enough to take me out
so you had to get help from your crew.
Greater is He that is in me
and He is more powerful than you.
He gives you permission to tempt a while
but you do not have the power to kill.
God steps in when He is ready
and tells the storm to be still.
You have been defeated
and there is no way that you can win.
I already have the victory
and do not have to be bound by sin.
You really messed up Satan
because you did not take me out.
God is my strength and protector
and that is what being His child is about.
You thought that you were hurting me
when you messed with some of my stuff.
You thought that I was going to give up
when the road got rough.
You meant it for evil
and tried to make me stumble.
God meant it for my good
so that I could get double for my trouble.

CHAPTER NINE

TELLING A
SOUR AND SWEET
STORY

ADAM AND EVE

One day Adam and Eve were hanging out LOLLIPOPing in the Garden of Eden. They were admiring God's handiwork when the serpent approached Eve. The serpent was Satan in the form of a snake. Satan was an angel who was TWIXed out of Heaven because he tried to become too powerful in God's kingdom. As a result of getting kicked out, he became RED HOT. He FLIPZ out and becomes NUTRAGEOUS because he is angry at God. He wants to cause MOUNDS of problems and CLUSTERS of worries for God's children as a way of getting back at Him. The serpent approached Eve and asked her if she wanted to eat some JUICY FRUIT off of one particular tree. She told him that the fruit looked BUBBLICIOUS and BUBBLE YUM but she was not supposed to touch that fruit or else she would die. The serpent convinced her that she would not die and finally got Eve to eat some of the fruit. Eve approached Adam and said let's TRIDENT and let's try that and Adam also ate some of the fruit. They began to SNACKWELL. I do not know if they ate the ORANGE SLICES, CHOCOLATE CHERRIES, CHERRY BLIMPS, or LEMON DROPS. Whatever it was, they were not supposed to eat off of that particular tree.

After they ate the fruit, they noticed that they were naked. They felt like MILKDUDS in a CRUNCH. They covered themselves with FIG NEWTON leaves. God called out to Adam and he tried to make a FAST BREAK because he was naked and ashamed. Nobody can make a SWEET ESCAPE from God, no matter where they go. It does not matter if they go to ANDES, MARS, the MILKWAY, or even in YORK. God asked Adam how did he know that he was naked. He asked him if he ate some of the JUICY FRUIT off of the forbidden tree. Adam said BUTTERFINGER was the finger that made me eat the fruit. Adam said it was the SWEETART that You gave me that made me eat the fruit. Eve responded and said that it was that SUCKER serpent that made her eat the fruit. Because of their disobedience, God put a curse on Adam, Eve and the serpent. That was the fall of man.

Everyone born after Adam and Eve was born into a world of sin. Just because we live in a sinful world does not mean that we have to be bound by sin. We will have to suffer trials and TASTETATIONS but everyone has a choice in how we will live our lives. We can be SOURHEADS and continue to be bound by SINFUL DELIGHTS or we can be JOLLY RANCHERS and accept Christ as the LIFESAVER of the world. Everyone who accepts God can experience a life of GOOD AND PLENTY, in spite of our sinful nature. Christians can live life abundantly NOW AND LATER in a land that is flowing with milk and A BIT OF HONEY. Weeping may endure for a night but ALMOND JOY comes in the morning.

THE SWEETEST BIRTHDAY PARTY

With Christmas and the New Year approaching, I wanted to make sure that everyone knows that Jesus is the reason for the season. It is not about Santa Claus, presents, reindeer, or even mistletoe. Christmas is about celebrating the birth of Jesus Christ and I thought it would be fitting to have a birthday party for Him.

The story began a long time ago when Baby Jesus was born in a manger. I did not say BABY RUTH, I said Baby Jesus. There was a big STARBURST in the sky and that is how the wise men found their way. It was the STARLIGHT MINTS that showed them the MILKYWAY. When they finally arrived, the PARTY MIX was on. No, I was not at that party but I will be at this year's celebration.

There will be singing, shouting, and dancing at the birthday party. We are featuring a live band called the REESES PIECES. I do not know what the latest dances are but I think people will be doing the TOOTSIE ROLL, the PECAN ROLL, the LOLLIPOP, the POPCORN, and the KIT KAT. If you cannot do any of these dances, I know that people are still doing the holy dance. Because when I think of His goodness and what He has done for me, I could dance all night. There will also be a DJ who will be spinning records. You are welcome to bring your LOLLIPOPs and CINNAMON DISKs. (LPs and CDs).

I know that CHOCOLATE CHERRIES will not go to a PARTY MIX unless food is being served. Do not worry about what you should eat because there will be GOOD and PLENTY. You will be able to SNACKWELL at the party. For those of you who are into fast food, we will be serving WHOPPERS. For those on a strict protein diet, we will be serving JELLY BEANS and NUT GOODIES. For those of you who are into daily bread, we will provide SWEETARTS and ROLOS with BUTTERFINGERS. If you are a vegetarian, we will be serving JUICY FRUIT that includes: LEMON DROPS, CHERRY BLIMPS, and ORANGE SLICES. The vegetable of the day will be CANDY CORN. I believe Ms. BRACHS will be doing all of the cooking and I know that she likes to SPICE DROPS her food. I almost forgot to tell you that all drinks are on the house. We will have an abundance of living water served in REESES CUPS. If you are into mixed drinks, the special of the evening will be milk with a BIT OF HONEY.

I know that some people will not attend a party unless they know who is coming. Everyone is invited to this birthday celebration. I am asking that you RSVP so we will know how many to prepare for. I have already heard from the WERTHERS, the TWIZZLERS, the SKITTLES, RUSSELL STOVER, PEPPERMINT PATTIE, MR. GOODBAR and his JUNIOR MINTS, the SIXLETS, the NUGGETS and their ASSORTED MINIATURES, the M&M's, and the BUTTONS. Some people have decided to be GUMMY BEARS and not attend the celebration. Those people are the ZAGNUTS, the CIRCUS PEANUTS, the CHERRY SOURS, the LEMONHEADS, the JAW BREAKERS, the SUCKERS, the NERDS, the SOURHEADS, the CRUNCHES, and the MILKDUDS.

Of course, you will need to know where the party is going to be held. You will not have to make a SWEET ESCAPE or a FASTBREAK to MARS, the ANDES, or even to YORK. The party is going to be held at the local church and you know that the church is in your heart. There is no cover charge so you will not have to set aside any money at PAYDAY. We want everyone to come and celebrate the LIFESAVER'S birthday. By the way, the guests of honor will be the THREE MUSKETEERS. (The Father, the Son, and the Holy Ghost) All we request of you is to be a JOLLY RANCHER and R.S.V.P.

If you are wondering what the dress code is, please come as you are.

CHAPTER TEN

INTIMACY WITH JESUS

I SPENT THE DAY WITH JESUS

I said to the Lord, there is something I want to do.
I want to spend my Saturday hanging out with You.
I need to feel Your presence and I want to feel Your touch.
I long to spend some uninterrupted time with You very much.
He answered me and said that all I had to do was ask.
We can set that day aside and together we will bask.
Early Saturday morning, He woke me with a gentle kiss.
I looked forward to that day and I was full of bliss.
I thanked Him for keeping me safe during the night.
Since I was in His presence, I knew everything was all right.
He told me that He had been waiting to spend this time with me.
He had so much in store and all I had to do was taste and see.
I was excited because I meditated on every word that He said.
The next thing I knew, He served me breakfast in bed.
I had previously read the menu and I remembered what it said.
On a special platter, He presented my daily bread.
Not only did He prepare it; He fed it to me as well.
With that kind of treatment, I knew my day would be swell.
We had our morning meditation and finished our sup.
He cleared away the dishes and said it was time to get up.
It was time for my personal hygiene, which takes about an hour.
The first thing on my list of things to do was get in the shower.
The water cleansed me physically from my head down to my toe.
As a result of asking forgiveness, He cleansed my mind and soul.
I started the day off right, refreshed with a clean slate.
I wondered what was next and I could hardly wait.
I was impatient and my anxiety made me feel a bit odd.
He gently told me to be still and know that He was God.
The blessings that He had in store, I did not want to miss.
He promised that they were only for me and I could count on this.
He is not slack concerning His promise and I do not have to thirst.
All of these things will be given to me, if I seek Him first.
After He reassured me, it was time to put on my clothes.
I did not know what to put on but He did because He always knows.
He told me in His word that I should not worry about what to wear.
He told me to put on the full armor even though He would be there.

He wanted me to be covered from my head down to my feet.
He told me to be ready if Satan and I would meet.
After I got dressed, it was time to read His book.
He told me to study myself approved and His word we began to look.
I wondered what lesson He had in store; He told me to taste and see.
He boldly shared that there would be no other gods before Me.
He is very jealous and wants first place in my heart.
That was my first lesson and that is how our study did start.
We turned over to 1 John that dealt with forgiveness, you see.
I must forgive others in order for Him to forgive me.
We looked in Romans that dealt with loving one other.
He told me to be kind to my sisters and brothers.
I cannot recall all of the scriptures but I know there was a bunch.
He said hide the word in my heart; it was time for us to eat lunch.
I offered to fix Him something but He insisted that I rest awhile.
I was beginning to see that Jesus knew how to treat a lady with style.
I did not have many groceries; He told me to take a seat.
I did not know what He was going to fix us to eat.
I apologized for not having much and He looked at me and said,
you remember what I did with two fish and five loaves of bread.
Lunch was great, we had plenty and afterwards I said,
when we finish our dessert, I want to relax in the bed.
I thanked Him for the food and our conversation was very deep.
I started to doze off but He does not slumber nor sleep.
Not only was He guarding me but the angels were watching me too.
I slept for a couple of hours and He woke me up about two.
When I opened my eyes, He sweetly smiled at me.
I wanted Him to know that I was as peaceful as I could be.
I worshipped and praised Him the best way that I could.
I wanted to let Him know that He had been so good.
I shouted hallelujah and did not know when my praise would end.
I had to let Him know that He was my lover and my best friend.
I also thanked Him for never leaving me alone.
The praise got so good to me that all I could do was moan.
But most of all, I thanked Him for saving a wretch like me.
If it was not for Him, I do not know where I would be.

Time went by fast because I was with my best friend.
I looked at the clock and it was time to eat again.
I wanted to bless the food before we sat down and ate.
He told me once again that He was going to fix my plate.
He handed it to me and it was piled with alot of stuff.
He served me food that I did not like and the meat was kind of tough.
I picked through my plate because I wanted to see
why He gave that kind of food to me.
He told me that if He left the plate-fixing up to me
that I probably would not eat food that was healthy.
He knows what is best and the food He served was nutritious.
I took a couple of bites and found it to be kind of delicious.
I thought I knew what I didn't like but I enjoyed it very much.
After I ate what would make me strong, He sweetened it just a touch.
I finished everything on my plate and it was not that bad.
I thanked Him for the food and for the conversation that we had.
I got up from the table and turned on the TV.
He turned it off and said that you need to spend this time with Me.
We had a long conversation about how far we had come.
He told me not to forget where He had brought me from.
I wanted to know when we could spend some intimate time again.
He said that He was available whenever I needed a friend.
Instead of getting caught up in all the things that we think please us,
clear your calendar and spend an intimate day with Jesus.

CHAPTER ELEVEN

MY LIFE-STORY

MY LIFE

my birth my breath my cry
my mom my hug my embrace
my kiss my cuddle my love
my food my relief my nap
my dismissal my exit my home
my family my environment my experiences
my birthday my attention my growth
my school my friends my education
my sisters my toys my buddies
my mom my queen my world
my dad my fear my pain
my trembling my shaking my nerves
my graduation my certificate my transfer
my junior high my friends my teachers
my homework my sports my activities
my puberty my anxieties my worries
my education my graduation my certificate
my high school my friends my growth
my temptations my pressures my mistakes
my boyfriend my trials my tribulations
my hiding my escaping my lies
my hair my shoes my clothes
my pain my mask my depression
my grades my parents my curfew
my curiosity my experiments my problems
my disappointments my heartache my pain
my mistakes my errors my tears
my pregnancy my baby my abortion
my low self-esteem my suicide attempt my goodness
my decisions my time my future
my grounding my restriction my punishment
my struggles my pain my running
my guilt my sorrow my shame
my struggles my fears my graduation
my junior college my freedom my wild side
my classes my work study my friends

my low self-esteem my parties my friends
my cover-up my clothes my drinking
my education my dorm-room my finances
my parties my parties my parties
my ego my pride my searching
my grades my drinking my tutor
my struggles my victories my graduation
my associates degree my completion my transfer
my university my adjustments my stress
my girls my drinking my parties
my classes my professors my extra-credit
my parents my headaches my decisions
my scholarship my financial aid my money
my car my apartment my bills
my lessons my discipline my graduation
my celebration my family my bachelor's degree
my job search my church my counselor
my stress my decisions my education
my goals my dreams my desires
my family my friends my support
my low self-esteem my boyfriend my hiding
my pressures my resentments my anger
my attitude my hurt my pain
my classes my job my money
my church my attendance my reasons
my support my best friends my gods
my education my growth my experience
my discipline my hard work my graduation
my celebration my stress my master's degree
my grandma my pain my goodness
my real job my relocation my opportunity
my skills my growth my progress
my foundation my transfer my relocation
my new job my stress my strain
my support my best friends my family
my boyfriend my hurt my pain
my tears my depression my nerves
my craziness my mistakes my insanity

my depression my isolation my separation
my relief my hiding my escaping
my mind my body my soul
my church my confession my salvation
my morals my values my beliefs
my clean heart my clean mind my soul
my relationship my fellowship my bible
my hunger my thirst my meditation
my growth my progress my tasks
my tears my depression my pain
my sin my mistakes my control
my backsliding my relapse my business
my heartache my suffering my tribulations
my confession my forgiveness my surrender
my second chance my clean slate my restoration
my fellowship my relationship my position
my studying my meditation my obedience
my sacrifices my hearing my doing
my blessings my blessings my blessings
my Father my Lord my Savior
my Jesus my Christ my Master
my hope my power my shelter
my victory my joy my peace
my healing my deliverance my security
my choice His will my decision
my God my God my God
my life my life my life

FRESHEN UP

I was caught up in sin, living a very ARRID extra dry lifestyle.

There were many times that I had to TUSSY with Satan.

He was causing the DEGREEs of heat to rise in my life.

He also caused HIGH ENDURANCE of problems for me.

I almost gave up but I surrendered my life to the RIGHT GUARD.

I was vulnerable and weak and asked God to become my POWERSTICK.

He wiped my tears SOFT & DRY and gave me a CRYSTAL CLEAN slate.

I no longer have to fight my own battles because God has ARM & HAMMERed Satan and BANned him from destroying my life.

My God is SUAVE and will always be my number one LADY'S CHOICE.

It is no SECRET what God can do.

I am SURE that what He has done for me, He can do the same thing for you.

ABOUT THE AUTHOR

Born and raised in Salina, Kansas, LaShawn Childs accepted Christ at the early age of nine. After completing high school, LaShawn received a Master's degree in Community Counseling. She is married to Carlester Childs and has two children, Cyle and Camille. LaShawn has taught adult Sunday school and youth bible classes. She has been the featured speaker at women's conferences. Together with her husband, she has presented godly relationship seminars, evangelism workshops, and taught vacation bible school. She is now using her gift of poetry to share God's healing power with the world.